by

Michael Mazyck

Dorrance Publishing Co
585 Alpha Drive
Pittsburgh, PA 15238
Visit our website at *www.dorrancebookstore.com*

ISBN: 979-8-8860-4123-1
eISBN: 979-8-8860-4788-2

Journey
Through
Life
and Love

So peaceful, so quiet, so calm, so sweet
I sit here and think while I watch you sleep
So selfish, so greedy, as you cuddle closer for warmth
Funny how your little hand clamps to me with such force
The sunlight beaming down on your face from the window
Will be the symbol of my promise to you
No matter how much it rains, or hard much the wind blows
My love for you will be absolute
Take these words and etch them for me
On your heart and in your mind
Blood of my blood, no matter how stormy
I will be there for you until the end of my life
Compelled, like the water, to obey the moon
I'll be the wave that can carry you
Even though you will no doubt outgrow these arms soon
I don't ever want to let you down
Life gets rough, and you might find yourself covered
Tumbling out of control after you get pulled under
Or maybe even get washed up on shore
To a place you've never been before
Just know that I'm here in any way I can be
All you have to do is reach out your hand
No matter how strong the current that pulls me
I'll make my way back to you on dry land

Sleep, my love, and I hope you dream sweet dreams
Dreams of rain and sand and shining sun
And our nights between the sheets
Dream of time being on our side, and freedom to just be
And possibilities as endless as the sky above the sea

Eyes that steal your gaze and draw you in
What you were looking at, now gone
Now come face to face with an angel
Beautiful emerald, delicate stone
Pierce into my very being and hook me in this place
Powerless to move or blink or say anything
I'm captive, but I like the way you like to captivate
My everything with just one look and redesign my fate
Destined to chase after them, those eyes that tore me down
And opened up a world for me I had never known til now
You snatched me up and I feel no shame
Drawn to you like a moth to flame
You've blessed me and now I reminisce on the moment everyday
Eyes that stole my gaze
Trapped like prey caught in a net
Afraid until I realized
The calm, and then they met
My lips and yours
What a turn of events
Passion whirling, swirling round
Levitating, I held you as we floated to the ground
A mystery, that look that changed it all; a single view
Love at first sight turned out so right because who I saw was you

I look away, ashamed to hear her say my name
Who wouldn't be? As the atmosphere slowly starts to turn to gray
It's hard to see, for me, when there are tears streaming down her face
And hard to be, when I am what she wants but I don't want to stay
Maybe the issue isn't really what I said before
But if this is love, why is my mind so ready to close the door?
In this love, should I really feel like I want something more?
And is this love? I wonder as she lays there on the floor
Anything for you, but be the one you want from me
But still, I try to please and be the man
You keep saying you want to see
I can be that hero who comes to fight away the demons
But when darkness falls on someone else, I want to be there too
I'm not wrong, but who's to say that what I think is right?
Right or wrong, these questions snatch my sleep away each night
While I lay next to you, silently continuing this fight
Neither wants to feel the shadow of the pain that comes tomorrow
When those words are said, and we are left to contemplate the sorrow

How sweet the taste of you will be
when I finally have you here with me
my love, I've waited oh so long
to hold you close inside this home

The snow outside did make it hard for me to find you but
it was destiny and love combined that reunited us
"at last," I think, "we're on our way," as I look at you and smile
your body sliding through the snow, leaving red across the ground

It was fate, it seems, that brought you back to where you broke my heart
but love my dear, will keep you here, after all this time apart

How I've missed those deep brown eyes that now fill up with tears
and the sound of your angelic voice, the music to my ears

A symphony of sounds created from your muffled screams
provides the perfect lullaby as I lay you down to sleep

Relax my dear, and close your eyes, it will all be over soon
let me bask in your warmth one final time,
as blood pours from your wounds

My love for you is never ending; I promise that's the truth
but if I'm honest, if it's not me, then no one will have you

All this time, I've been here burning, in the destruction of your wake
until tonight, when I rise a phoenix, from the ashes of love's flames.

Michael Mazyck

Again, we've run out, and again you must go
Again, I sit here craving you, again all alone
Merciless. It steals away any chance to get too close
Tonight was yet another example of almost
We almost had enough to meet face to face
But almost is almost always too late
It will pay for its crimes, were I to discover
A way to get even, for the sake of my lover
I'll catch it, and shackle its hands to a wall
And batter it senseless, once and for all
Time, when you're mine, I will be crowned
The victor, at last, and as your blood trickles down
Your face, I hope you count every minute
As we did, awaiting a break from your limits

I never lied, I love you in a place where there's no space and time
I'm paralyzed, it's still hard to speak whenever you're around it's like
I'm terrified, to let you know that's what I feel right now
But know I'm mesmerized, because my heart is yours and there's no doubt
That one Ab Soul line opens a path for my
Words and my thoughts; addiction grabs hold like
My hand on your thigh, I wish I had more time
And hands, so I could cover you up with my
Caress, that I hope is gentle enough
Except for the times when you ask for it rough
My queen, I just thought I should let you know
That I love you, and wherever you are, I will go

It's quiet. The sounds of the creek are soothing as we stare up at the moon. We lock eyes. Both of us can tell what the other is thinking but neither wants to say a word. I have to go. The words that should've been said ages ago, but it's hard to leave your side. Longing. The overwhelming feeling that I can't suppress every time I let you leave my sight. Guilt. Both of us want this to never end, but does that make this wrong, or right? Lust. When our lips touch there's a primal urge, an undeniable force that hungers for your flesh and nothing else will satisfy it. Peace. What it feels like when you're finally with me again, away from them, and in my arms. Time. Just a second alone in your presence is all I need but still somehow not nearly enough. Crave. Your hair, your smile, your lips, your skin, your soul. Power. My warrior who needs nothing and no one; your strength draws me to you perhaps even more than all your other features. My wolf's bane. Beautiful, elegant, dangerous flower, I accept your poison. Closer. Afflict me if you must, with leaves and petals that are deadly; but know that I'll come closer still, my flower, if you let me.

Those devious eyes, those persuasive lips, those perilous thighs and voluptuous hips, are hooks, are nets, and they've pulled me in; I'm wrapped around her fingertips. With all my strength I've fallen victim; this sinister sweetness brought me down; apparently she's my only weakness and whatever she wills is my fate now. Delicate like a tender lily, fierce just like a wolverine, a fearsome but lovely combination, a beautiful sight, a wondrous scene. A toxic bite, a gentle kiss, the feel of her moistened, soft pink lips, makes it hard for me, and I must admit that I have no desire to resist. As I uncover all her treasure, bring pleasure to her every nerve, she can't find the words to thank me, so she grants me what she thinks I deserve. Her body is a palace and I explore its passageways, find all its deepest, darkest corners and make them see the light of day. Like the most exotic fruit is the taste of her heavenly palace walls, and I feast until they come to ruin, until they tremble before me and fall. Her power has turned to mine, it seems, but either way it was like a dream; like I drank from the fabled fountain and gained immortality.

Slowly but surely, I'm falling, I'm stumbling, tumbling, fumbling out of control. And it's hard to admit the reason is you but I'm sure by now you know the truth. You're the day to my night, the mate for my soul, the reason I never again want to be alone; don't leave me alone, just stay here forever, and I promise the days will keep getting better. You make me more than what I am, in any way, in every way, and every day I know your name I consider myself blessed. Those three little words I want to say, that step into the future I want to take, and that leap of faith I want to make, are all grounded by my fears. But into the skies now I take flight with you, with strength that alone I never knew, the two of us together, falling and flying, into a love that is deep and undying.

The lights are blinding
Music and fanfare fill the ballroom
And as they all dance and drink the night away I find myself searching
For the eyes that found mine the last time we were here
The same eyes that picked me apart and stole my tongue
I was powerless under their gaze and I loved every second of it
What kind of creature she must be, to so effortlessly ensnare me
 Proud as I am, and leave me there, helpless and craving more
I have resolved that tonight, here at this masquerade
I will find this goddess and she will receive my praise
And then I spot her.
The lights dim to nothingness and the music fades to silence
And all I can see in the room is her
Dressed in all black, she elegantly makes her way down the stairs,
Eyes locked on mine, penetrating to the depths of all that I am
And as my heart tries to tear out of my chest, I make myself move
Forward, toward this wonder, this specimen of excellence until
Here we are, face to face, staring, unblinking
Three lifetimes go by as we stand there, not saying a word
And then I reach for it. The mask hiding what I wasn't ready to see
A smile and lips that rob me of my will to do anything else but
Keep them to myself for all eternity. What happened next
Was not a conscious choice, but as I drop her mask onto the floor
I find my hand taking hers and when I come back to Earth
My lips are on hers and her hands are holding me tightly
The softest, smoothest things I have ever felt
Please don't ever let this moment end
My only thoughts now are never wanting to stop, and worry
About what she will find when she unmasks what is now a shell

Michael Mazyck

Of a man once proud, and strong, and loving
What will this goddess think when she sees that I have given so much
That the me I once was exists now only in pieces?
A single tear makes its way down my face
    and before I can turn away, ashamed
She gently wipes it away and her smile takes away my will to leave
She takes my hand in hers as if to say she understands
And leads me away, and I follow helplessly, unsure of what else to do
The sun is coming up and still her aura is blinding
And as we walk through the sand all I hear is the roar of my own heartbeat

The roar of my heartbeat fades away as the world comes back into view
But despite the sunrise, the sand, the sea, all I can see is you
Your long, thick braid complements your brown skin
Your hips in that dress as it blows in the wind
And that smile you smile as you emerge from the ocean
Combine to create your hypnotic potion
A vision, glistening, flawlessly floating,
Towards me…I'm nervous, defenseless, and open
I feel like I'm soaring through the sky on a cloud
Right next to an angel with her wings spread wide now
If it happens to be wrong then at least it felt right
To experience you up close, to be able to take flight
My darling, through cacophony, you are all that I heard
So I will take it as a sign and I will love you until it hurts
And then another day longer I'll pour out my heart
To fill up your cup, no matter how hard
This life has been meaningless without you in it
So I thank you, sweet angel; now my search is finished

Sweet vanilla scented flower, may I watch you for an hour? It's just that you're so enchanting, so compelling with your power. Let me gaze upon your splendor, on your beauty, on your grace, while you're basking in the golden warmth that's covering this place. And oh, how your aroma tends to fill me up and take me home, to the perfect place where you and I can leave the world and be alone. Alone...yes, I alone, will be keeper of your effervescence, and in doing so I'll feed your glow and never have to leave your presence. In the night ill wish sweet dreams to you before I go to sleep and in the morning, greet you with a smile before I'm on my feet. You'll smile that beautiful, silent smile that special way you do, and send me to a deeper depth of more in love with you. Sweet vanilla scented flower, while I watch you for an hour, could you do me just one favor? Never let the rain or the clouds keep you down, or take away your power. Neither cold nor pest could make you anything less than what you truly are: sweet flower, if you were anything else, you would truly be a star.

Your skin is lava on my fingertips, your body burns as I kiss your lips, your flames engulf me, squeeze me, as I fire dance between your hips. Look into my eyes, I want to see your pleasure rise, like how I feel the warmth, the moisture increasing on your thighs. You climb on top, like an equestrian master, first you ride slow and then you ride faster, and faster until you wear yourself out, and I feel trickling from your river mouth. And for a moment you pause, without a scream or a shout, while you tremble above me, eyes closed and open mouth, until I sit up and sink my teeth into your neck and push as deep inside as your body lets me get. Then onto your back I throw you, your claws tearing me apart, but I love the pain from you getting pleasure, and our secrets in the dark. Off of the bed we roll, down to the floor and again I am on top, as you moan my name and scream for more, encore, please don't stop. You pull me closer and I find myself cuffed, by your iron grip, but it's not tight enough, as I pick you apart with my master key, make you overflow uncontrollably. I find myself swimming in your satisfaction, in the deep end, what a fatal attraction, but a chance I'm always willing to take and a mistake even, that I'm willing to make.

Fireworks is all I can say to describe the feelings, to describe the tastes on the tip of my tongue, I'm hungry for none other than you while we hide inside from the sun. Under cover of nightfall the dark hinders our vision but the sounds and sensations of every collision are clear as day, though the sun won't shine in the places I touch when I make you mine. I'm not so sure how discrete we can be, for the sounds of your screams and their frequency are audible to all in range of our performance, as the bed floats up, and away, and the floor hits. Cry out for me, scream my name, let your nails paint a picture as we ignite this flame. Tear me apart, my vicious vixen, and I'll accept the pain while I feed my addiction. Explosions of pleasure, waves of emotion, the satisfaction from swimming in your ocean, is almost too much for my body to bear, almost...then I grab a fistful of your hair. You squeeze me tighter and your body drips as if it's melting away while I kiss your lips, pure fireworks, our fire burns, despite the rainfall pouring down.

The screaming silence is deafening, and this emptiness is filling,
Is chilling like the cold of space, like this bed, a lonely empty place.

There's nothing here but nothingness, without your kiss, your soft caress,
Come stay with me and give me peace; please rid me of my restlessness.

The feel of your skin, your dazzling blue eyes, the way your smile
sparkles and shines,
It's insane to me how easily you became my moon when all I saw was night.

The earth could stop spinning, the sun could stop shining,
The seas could dry up while the stars are colliding,

And still all I would need is you and I,
To be my world and complete my life.

Michael Mazyck

Her fury, harsh like a raging storm
Whips wind around, and branches are torn
From trees around for centuries
Her power is immense, but doesn't scare me
Despite the debris pelting my skin
And clouds blocking the sun so no light will come in
To me, I see Heaven when I look in her eyes
So I reach for her hand to clear the dark from her skies
I pull her in close, so she knows I am here
To weather any storm, conquer any fear
To be the provider of any desire
And quiet her raging with the strength of my fire

Soft lips meet with mine
This feeling is amazing
She likes heavy rain

Drops drip down her face
Trickling down her flawless skin
I am her captive

Chains of affection
Binding me and seal my fate
The warden of love

I'm ashamed to say my dear, that I
Have neglected to serenade you with soft lines
And words, that tell of your infinite beauty
And describe all the ways you bring happiness to me
From your mind, sharp, and quick, and inspired
To your lips so soft, the doorway to my desires
You embody the things I have craved for so long
Sometimes I find myself wanting to write a love song
A like song maybe, since maybe love is too soon
Accompanied by notes on a keyboard in bad tune
Just so you come to put your fingers on mine
To once again create a moment that is frozen in time
So many memories over so few days
The fuel for the pen that writes on this page
The inspiration for the things that from now on I'll do
Is totally, unequivocally because of you

Your scent lingers here
Dark brown skinis mixed with light
Beautiful union

I want what is mine
Circumstance is in the way
Will she wait for me?

Queen deserves the best
This peasant will win her hand
I will serve her well

The day will soon come
True, time waits for no man, but
For her it will bow

She's an expert at the demolition of the walls around my heart
She charms her way into the cracks then slowly breaks them all apart
Now I'm paralyzed, and she's left me defenseless
I'm head over heels and out of touch with my senses
Cause all I see and think is her; she's stolen my heart;
    what a beautiful curse
Every moment with her is like pure magic; every moment without is
    utterly tragic
And I find myself dreaming, wishing for her,
    against my will and out of habit
I'm borderline unstable, and can't be too far from insane
But when I hold her hands in mine, we become the eye of the hurricane
I smile at her smile and stare into her eyes,
    those damn green eyes that hypnotize
What a wicked shade of mind control, but I love it and I need it to survive
Together we are the perfect pair, apart we slowly self-destruct
Like time bombs waiting to explode or volcanoes waiting to erupt
Together, like the land and sea, the two of us are really one
You've broken in and finally our masterpiece is truly done

Lonely nights and sad eyes. She's alone in bed again, the space between her thighs just above her knees missing the presence of my warm hand.

Noisy chirps and subtle creaks. The incessant sound of the crickets outside doesn't even register to her as she ponders, deep in reflection.

Frozen clocks and restless thoughts. She can't help but feel like time has come to a complete stop and life is taking full advantage of the opportunity by shoveling on more stress.

Weary hearts and warm moonlight. She struggles with the distance, but as she clutches his camouflage hoodie, she lets out a sigh of relief and stares up at the full moon, realizing he might be close enough to see it too.

Foggy windows and bright lights. It's morning now, and as the faucet in the kitchen drips every few seconds she gazes at the golden chandelier and tries to imagine where in the deep blue sea he might be.

Sunny skies and tan lines. She walks outside to go to her car and looks at her silver watch to check the time. Suddenly, the sun gets so much warmer and the biggest smile forms on her face.

One more day until she's on vacation. One more day until she leaves this place. One more day until he's on the beach with her, staring at her gentle face.

She looks down at her fingers, and the spaces in between, and remembers how he promised he would come back from sea.

Happy endings and evening strolls
Barefoot walking on dusty roads
Moonlight dances and cloudless skies
Tears of joy and big brown eyes.

Michael Mazyck

Why should I dream, when perfection lies, in my bed next to me;
    why close my eyes?
Not a fantasy, not a wish on a star, could give me a woman more amazing
    than you are,
Could bring me happiness in the way that you do,
    or find an explanation for how I love you.
A single reason I cannot give, for why I never want to live
A life without you every waking minute;
    my world is a wasteland without you in it.
Take my heart in both your hands and hold it to your chest;
Squeeze it tight and give me life; I want to feel you in every breath.
In and out goes the air in my lungs,
    while love fills my soul and my mind starts to run
Run wild with the thought of you by my side, forever and always,
    to our future we stride.

25

26